101 Wacky facts about MUMMIES

By Jack C. Harris

Illustrated by Bryan Hendrix

A Parachute Press Book

SCHOLASTIC INC.

New York Toronto London Aukland Sydney

ISBN 0-590-44889-7
Copyright © 1991 by Parachute Press Inc.
All rights reserved. Published by Scholastic Inc.

Designed by Paula Jo Smith

12 11 10 9 8 7 6 5 4 3   1 2 3 4 5 6/9

Printed in the U. S. A.   01

First Scholastic printing, July 1991

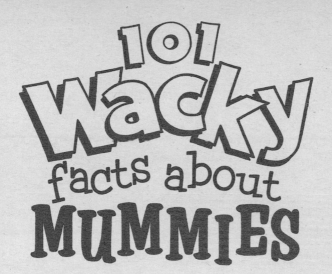

101 Wacky facts about MUMMIES

WILL THE REAL
MUMMY PLEASE
LIE DOWN?

6

DID YOU KNOW that even though some mummies are thousands of years old, many of them still have their fingernails and toenails? Some of them even have their eyelashes!

What is a mummy anyway? Are they found only in Egypt? Follow us and unwrap mummy mysteries!

A mummy is a human being or animal preserved and protected from decaying after death. There are three ways a dead body can become mummified: by freezing, by drying, or, as the ancient Egyptians did, by using secret chemicals.

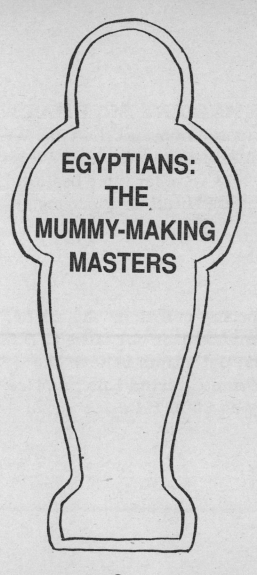

EGYPTIANS:
THE
MUMMY-MAKING
MASTERS

FOR ANCIENT EGYPTIANS death was more important than life! Why? Because death lasted longer than life! So tombs were far more beautiful than the houses built for the living!

Egyptians practiced the art of mummification for close to 5,000 years! Scientists believe the Egyptians started this practice as early as 3000 B.C.

11

THERE IS NO MUMMY-MAKING handbook! Maybe it was considered too sacred to write down, but only a few descriptions of mummy-making have been found.

The earliest known Egyptian mummies were not wrapped in cloth but were dried out naturally after being buried in the hot, dry, and sandy ground of Egypt. (They weren't just trying to get a tan on the beach, that's for sure!)

Egyptian legend said that King Osiris was the first to be mummified. The story claimed that Anubis, an Egyptian god with the head of a jackal, embalmed the king himself. King Osiris then became King of the Underworld and all Egyptians wanted to join him after death.

No one knows *exactly* what secret ingredients the Egyptians used for preserving their mummies. But scientists now believe that the ingredients included oil of cedar (similar to today's turpentine) and natron, a mineral with a high salt content.

What do you get when you unwrap the linen used on just one mummy and sew each strip together? A strip of linen that would reach up and down a football field four times!

The mummy of an Egyptian V.I.P. (very important person) had as many as twenty layers of wrappings!

In 1977, when Egyptian authorities discovered that the 3,000-year-old mummy of Pharaoh Ramses II was being invaded by beetles, the mummy was sent to France to be treated and cured by a team of scientists. Ramses II traveled to France with a passport stating his occupation as: "King—deceased."

WRAP SESSION!

MAKING A MUMMY was no easy job! It took centuries of trial and error to get it right. But once the Egyptians got the process right, they turned it into an art!

It took seventy days to prepare a mummy. It's creepy to think that embalmers almost lived with the mummy until it was laid to rest in its tomb!

Ancient Egyptians believed the heart, not the brain, was the center of intelligence and memory!

Although the internal organs were kept in jars and buried with the mummy, the brain was probably thrown away! The Egyptians considered the brain a minor organ!

Shake, rattle, and roll! When the Egyptians first mummified their dead, they left the brain intact. So when archaeologists moved them, they could hear the dried up brain rattle in the skull!

BRAIN MUSH! YUK! The Egyptians eventually removed the brain. To do this, a metal hook was pushed up through the nostril and moved back and forth until the brain became mushy and could be spooned out through an eye socket!

The left side of the body was slit open to remove the liver, lungs, stomach, and intestines. Each organ was preserved with natron in a separate container called a canopic jar.

When the tomb of Queen Hetepheres was discovered in 1925, her mummy had been stolen by grave-robbers, but her internal organs, kept in canopic jars, were found intact after 4,500 years!

For some unknown reason, Egyptian embalmers did not remove the kidneys.

IN THE EARLIEST MUMMIES, the heart of a person being mummified was left in place. However, in later years the heart was removed and embalmed like the other internal organs, and a stone scarab (or beetle) was put in its place.

Spices helped dry out the body and spice scents also kept the body from stinking up the tomb! You can imagine what a dead body smelled like in the hot desert weather!

Sometimes the wrapped-up body was covered in a black resin called pitch. This resin pitch was called "momia," therefore the origin of the word "mummy."

One pharaoh had small onions for eyes! Embalmers took great care with the mummy's eyes. Some of them would paint irises on the linen they used to stuff the eye sockets. Others used colored stones, or even onions!

Rich Egyptians wanted it all! Before being wrapped up, future mummies were adorned with all the jewels and gold they could take with them. The richer the Egyptian, the richer the mummy!

Some people wanted a paint job too! So Egyptian mummies were sometimes painted—yellow for women and red for men.

A MANICURE AND PEDICURE
for a mummy meant capping its
fingernails and toenails with gold!

**Sometimes female mummies were
buried with an extra wig. After all,
who would want to go to the Land
of the Dead without a change of
hairdo!**

THERE'S NO SUCH THING as a fat mummy . . . no matter how fat someone was when they were alive, the drying-out process put mummies on an instant diet!

It wasn't at all strange for fingertips, ears, or toes to fall off the mummy! These pieces were saved in jars and buried near the tomb, away from evil spirits.

The most sacred animal in ancient Egypt was Apis, the bull. It was believed that the god Apis was the creator of all gods. So bulls were not only mummified but given royal funerals!

Sometimes when a beloved pet cat died, a family would shave off their eyebrows to show just how sad they were . . . then the family cat would be mummified.

The Egyptians mummified crocodiles, birds and fish, and even insects and scorpions!

The mummy of the high priestess Makare was buried with another small mummy. Scientists assumed it was her baby until they X-rayed the mummy and found it wasn't a baby, but a baboon!

WHEN THE CATACOMB of jackals, a tomb full of mummified corpses of wild dogs, was discovered, the 2,000-year-old bones were so fragile they crumbled.

Archaeologists found an underground tomb that contained over a million mummified birds!

Hundreds of magical and protective amulets were tucked between the mummy's wrappings. Each amulet protected a certain part of the body. The heart scarab amulet was the most important, but other amulets portraying plants and animals, and even an eye amulet, were indispensable!

FARM TOOLS were sometimes secured inside a mummy-shaped figure called an ushabti. It was believed the ushabti would work the fields of King Osiris in the afterworld.

Even with mummification, Egyptian embalmers still feared evil spirits. To make sure that the spirits would recognize the body, the bound head was covered with a portrait mask. But each mask had a plaited beard resembling the beard of King Osiris!

PASSPORT PLEASE! For the Egyptians the Book of the Dead was like a passport or map that helped the dead person travel through dangerous areas of the underworld.

Egyptian artists painted eyes on the sides of coffins not just for decoration . . . but so the mummy could look out of the coffin. That's why for years mummies were placed in their coffins on their sides so they could see what was going on!

Many Egyptians had not one, but three coffins. Each coffin would fit into the other and was nailed shut forever . . . well almost.

THE FIRST
MUMMY-
WRAPPERS

IF YOUR FATHER was a mummy-maker, chances were you would be one too. In ancient Egypt the family business was handed down from father to son!

Embalmers lived in an area of their own. Poor people, who could never afford to be embalmed like the rich, considered embalmers repulsive people who made their living by handling the dead.

In many cases, it was the slaves and servants of the embalmers who actually did all the "dirty work."

While embalmers were well-paid and even rich, some would decorate the mummy with clay jewelry and keep the real jewels for themselves!

IN LATER YEARS, many embalmers became lazy and sloppy. Archaeologists have found mummies stuffed with broken-off limbs. Sometimes the feet were cut off so that the mummies would fit into smaller coffins.

What? Chicken bones! Mysterious extra bones found wrapped up with mummies baffled scientists, until they discovered they were probably just leftover bones from an embalmer's lunch!

TOMB IT MAY
CONCERN

45

EGYPTIAN WRITINGS CLAIM it took twenty years to build a single pyramid. The pharaohs usually started building their tombs as soon as they came to power.

No animals, please! Under the hot desert sun it was much too hot to have animals haul the heavy blocks used to build the pyramids. So all the work was done by men!

TWO MILLION blocks of stone were used to build each pyramid. Groups of workers would drag the cut stones up ramps of mud. New ramps were added as the pyramid grew.

The pyramids weren't built by slaves! On the contrary, workers were well-fed, well-housed, and well-paid.

Tombs with wooden beams were only for the wealthy since the few trees in Egypt made wood expensive.

The great pyramids of Egypt are nothing more than gigantic gravestones! Even though they took workers years to build, pyramids were used only to cover the tombs of pharaohs.

AN EGYPTIAN TOMB constructed for a pharaoh or other royalty wasn't just a grave. It was a fortress built to protect the pharaoh's treasure from grave-robbers.

Egyptians believed that the mummy's spirit could change into any shape, usually a bird, and fly through the stone walls of the tomb!

Booby traps, false doors, dead-end passages, and tunnels were built into the pyramids to prevent the tombs from being robbed. But millions of tombs were robbed anyway!

But how did the thieves find their way? It's believed that they would plot a robbery with a guard, a builder, even a priest or an embalmer, and then split the treasure!

Grave-robbing was a full-time job in Egypt. It was also a family business in which secrets were passed on from father to son!

Jewelry and furniture were made for the deceased. It all would be buried in the tomb. Carved statues of the dead person would serve as resting places for its spirit if anything happened to the mummy.

GRAVE-ROBBERS sometimes set mummies on fire to light up the tombs they looted!

Tired of being constantly robbed, the pharaohs began cutting small tombs in cliff walls and valleys. This began the tradition of the Valley of the Kings, an ancient burial site for Egyptian royalty for 500 years. Unfortunately, most of these tombs were robbed as well.

Around 1000 B.C. some Egyptian priests rewrapped many of the royal mummies disturbed by grave-robbers. They hid them in secret tombs other than those in the Valley of the Kings. These mummies are now impossible to identify.

Why is the "Smiling Mummy" smiling? Probably because she was discovered in 1989, untouched by looters, and is the oldest Egyptian mummy found to date— a mere 4,400 years old!

One mummy was found with a newspaper from 1944! Impossible but true. In 1944 a grave-robber was struck by a rock that fell from the ceiling, killing him instantly. When the tomb was found twenty-five years later, he was nothing but a skeleton. Scientists first thought they had discovered a robber as old as the mummy, but when they found the newspaper, the mystery was unwrapped!

FAREWELL,
MUMMY
DEAREST

MEMBERS OF EGYPTIAN royalty paid mourners to weep, tear their garments, and throw sand on their heads as they followed the funeral procession. Women mourners let out scary sorrowful cries to frighten the evil spirits away from the mummy.

The ancient Egyptians believed that the underworld—the Kingdom of the Dead—was exactly like the world above. They even believed that there was another Nile River flowing under the desert sand!

Buried alive! That was the fate of some servants of dead royalty. How else could they continue to serve in the afterlife? If they were lucky, they were killed first and then buried with their master's mummy.

Eventually, the families of the dead objected to having all their help killed to "join" the mummy. So the priests and embalmers decreed that paintings or statues of servants would serve just as well.

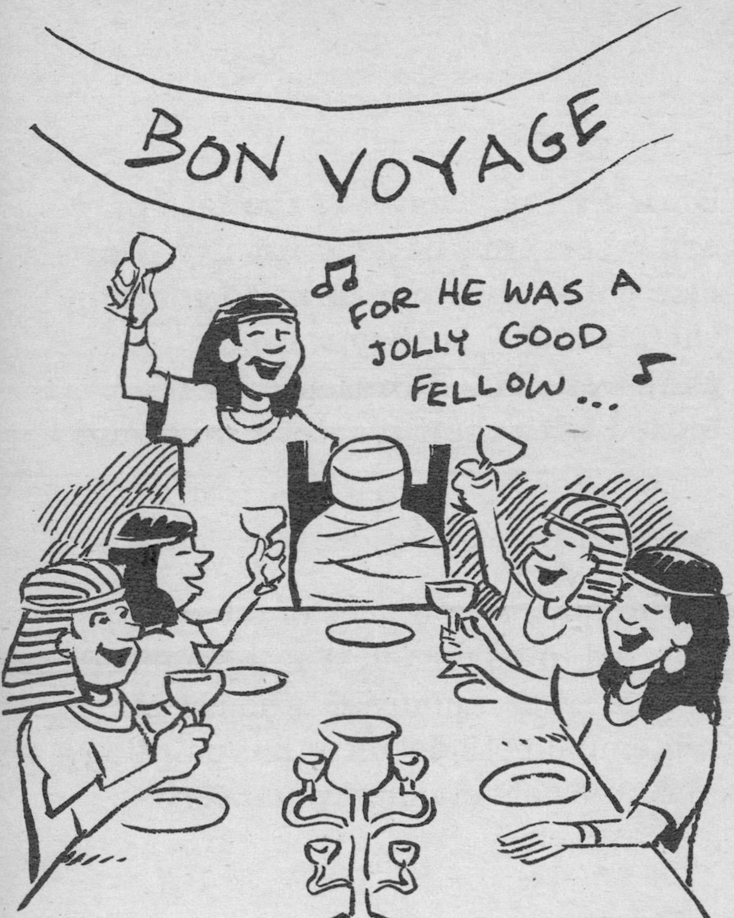
BON VOYAGE
FOR HE WAS A
JOLLY GOOD
FELLOW...

AT THE END of a funeral, a great feast was held in the tomb, and the mummy was the guest of honor! The mummy was taken out of its coffins and propped up while a priest performed an important ceremony called "The Opening of the Mouth." This ceremony, the Egyptians believed, permitted the mummy to speak, eat, and move in the afterworld . . . but, of course, no mouth was really opened because it was under layers and layers of wrappings!

Just in case the mummy wanted a snack, relatives would bring food to the tomb to feed the spirit of the mummy for months after their burial.

I WANT MY
MUMMY!

IN THE MIDDLE AGES, when Europeans discovered the existence of mummies, weird things started to happen. . . .

Poor Egyptians were eager to sell, and Europeans were eager to buy. . . . Mummy money-making went on successfully for close to 400 years.

From A.D. 1029 to 1291, when traders and warriors first brought news about Egyptian mummies back to Europe, people became convinced that the mummies held the key to eternal youth!

EUROPEANS BEGAN using the resin used to seal the ancient tombs as medicine. They called this medicine "mummy" . . . the secret to eternal youth.

Mummies were also boiled! As they boiled, the oils released by the mummy would be skimmed off the top. This "mummy oil" would be sold to treat bruises!

Or why not grind up a mummy and use the powder to treat an upset stomach!

MUMMIES WERE BIG BUSINESS
and there weren't enough mummies to
go around! So factories were set up in
Egypt to create instant mummies. Bodies of criminals, beggars, or dead animals were covered in pitch, quickly
dried in the desert sun, then ground
up into mummy powder!

Francis I, King of France in the 1500's, carried a pouch full of mummy powder in case he got into an accident and needed a quick remedy!

In the sixteenth century, Ambroise Paré, a French surgeon, published findings in his medical journal of the harmful effects of "mummy" medicine—and people finally stopped using it.

A POPULAR European social activity in the 1800's was "mummy unwrapping." Rich Europeans would buy a mummy from a trader, invite friends over, and unwrap the mummy during a party! Sometimes this could even be a dinner party where people would eat and drink while watching the bindings of a mummy being removed!

Egyptians thought the supply of mummies was endless, so they often ground up any they found and used them for fertilizer!

In the 1800's ancient mummy wrappings were shipped to papermills in the United States and used to make brown wrapping paper!

Sometimes poorer people's mummies were found in better condition than those of the rich. After all, who would be interested in a mummy without a treasure?

Thatch a roof with a mummy? Why not chop one up for firewood? Or panel your home with coffin wood! Egyptians found multiple uses for their mummies, that's for sure!

THE
CHINCHORRO
CONNECTION

DID YOU KNOW that the oldest mummy was not discovered in Egypt? Archaeologists found it in South America with the Chinchorro Indians of Chile! In fact the oldest Egyptian mummy is only 4,400 years old, while the oldest Chinchorro mummy is no less than 7,800 years old!

Chinchorro mummies didn't exactly rest in peace. They were buried standing up!

There are so many Chinchorro mummies that people in Arica, Chile, the modern city on the site of the ancient Indians' land, dig up a new mummy almost every time they stick a shovel in the ground!

For many years Europeans were believed to have infected the South American Indians with tuberculosis. But by studying Chinchorro mummies, scientists found out that some Chinchorros had died of the disease long before the Europeans arrived.

By studying mummies closely, scientists have discovered that Chinchorro men did a lot of deep-sea diving. How do they know that? Because many of the mummies showed that men had suffered from ear infections and deafness caused by heavy water pressure.

The Incas of Peru, neighbors of the Chinchorros, mummified their kings, placed them on thrones, and paraded them around on holidays!

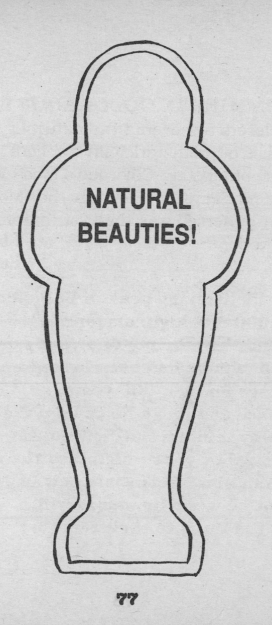

NATURAL
BEAUTIES!

MUMMIES IN COLORADO? When explorers discovered the naturally dried bodies of prehistoric cliff dwellers in none other than Colorado's Mesa Verde National Park, it was clear that Mother Nature herself was the first mummy-maker!

On the freezing peak of El Plomo, 18,000 feet high, explorers found the mummy of a young boy. Although he had been locked up in a cave for over 500 years, he looked as though he could wake up at any minute! But how could a young boy get so high into the mountains? Scientists now believe that he was a human sacrifice by the Incas to their Sun God.

WHERE CAN YOU FIND a pickled mummy? In the British Isles and Denmark of course! The peat bogs, a swamplike area made up of moss and water, contain acids that create the mummies by a process similar to pickling! Except the mummies aren't found in jars.

In the 1790's travelers discovered natural mummies frozen in the Aleutian Islands. Their internal organs had been removed and their bodies had been stuffed with moss and hay. The freezing weather preserved them for centuries.

In 1977 a 500-year-old Inuit burial site was discovered by scientists in Greenland. The eight naturally frozen mummies they found are now exhibited in a museum in Nuuk, Greenland.

The great Scottish seaman John Paul Jones, hero of the American Revolution, became an accidental mummy! When he died in Paris in 1792, his body was sealed in a lead coffin filled with alcohol to be shipped back to America. Instead he was buried in France and forgotten. When his coffin was discovered in 1905, his body was so well preserved that doctors recognized him from his portraits!

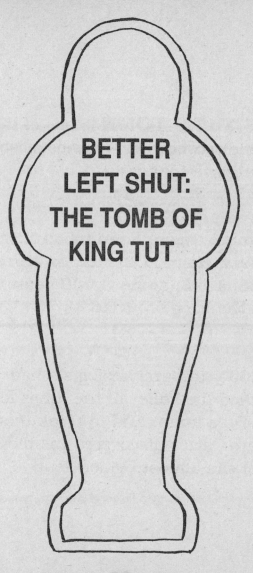

BETTER
LEFT SHUT:
THE TOMB OF
KING TUT

KING TUT'S TOMB is one of the few tombs discovered by archaeologists before grave-robbers!

The tomb was opened by an English explorer, Howard Carter, on November 26, 1922, some 3,000 years after the king's burial!

For 100 years archaeologists had searched the Valley of the Kings for King Tut's tomb. And to think that Howard Carter discovered the hidden burial site almost by accident!

In 1907, archaeologists had discovered pots from King Tut's funerary banquet and linen from his embalming process in the Valley of the Kings. They knew his tomb couldn't be too far away!

Howard Carter knew where he wanted to excavate but couldn't! Why? Because he would disturb tourist traffic! Finally, Howard Carter dug a short distance away from the pit where the pots and linens had been found. There he dug up the first of sixteen steps that would lead to the entrance of King Tut's tomb.

IT WAS A SHORT LIFE INDEED!
King Tut was nine years old when he
became pharaoh and died at the age of
eighteen.

**There were over 3,000 different
objects discovered in the tomb.
Howard Carter and his men spent
ten years cataloguing the treasures.**

The golden shrine containing King
Tut's mummy was almost 11 feet wide,
16-1/2 feet long and 9 feet high! It took
the explorers 84 days just to take the
shrine apart.

THE MOST INCREDIBLE
treasures were King Tut's coffins. The first two were gilded with gold and decorated with colored glass . . . but the third and last coffin was made of solid gold and weighed 296 pounds!

Over 143 pieces of jewelry were discovered inside the wrappings of King Tut's mummy!

Priceless treasures found in King Tut's tomb included his solid gold portrait mask; a jeweled cosmetic jar with a sculpted lion on top, sticking out its tongue; hundreds of gold figurines; an ebony child's chair inlaid with ivory; ornamental vases; fifteen gold and jeweled rings; and ear and neck ornaments.

🦋

King Tut planned to be busy in the underworld! Among the treasures in his tomb, the explorers found a boomerang, a forked stick for catching snakes, paddles for boats, robes, sandals, and arrows! Last but not least were enough seeds to plant a large garden!

Would you believe, as thousands did, that a golden typewriter with hieroglyphic characters was found in King Tut's tomb? Charles Langdon Clarke, reporter for the Toronto *Mail and Empire*, soon admitted it was a hoax!

!

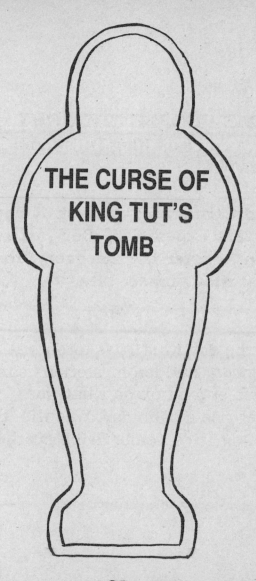

THE CURSE OF
KING TUT'S
TOMB

SOME PEOPLE THOUGHT there was a curse on King Tut's tomb when . . .

Lord Carnarvon, sponsor of Howard Carter's expedition, died just two months after the discovery from a mysterious insect bite.

On the day King Tut's tomb was opened a sudden mysterious sandstorm sprang up on what was otherwise a calm day. Was the "Curse of King Tut's Tomb" flying overhead?

Some of the Egyptian workers panicked on the day the tomb was first entered when a hawk, recognized as a symbol of Egyptian royalty, began slowly circling overhead.

The legend of the "Curse of King Tut" began because of Lord Carnarvon's sudden death after the tomb was entered and reports surfaced of a supposed inscription that read: "Death shall come on swift wings to defilers of the tomb. He shall sicken. He shall thirst." In fact, no such inscription was ever found!

CAN YOU HANDLE THIS STORY?

Count Louis Hamon, who owned the mummified hand of King Tut's sister-in-law, discovered after a while that the hand had become soft and pliable and seemed to actually bleed. While this was probably due to the expert embalming techniques of the ancient Egyptians, it frightened Count Hamon enough that he threw the hand into his fireplace. He claimed he then saw the spirit of a young Egyptian princess arise from the flames!

WHERE DOES THE MUMMY

of King Tut rest today? Even though his treasures are on display at the Cairo Museum, King Tut himself still lies in his tomb, exactly where he was discovered in 1922! Who knows, maybe the Egyptian government fears the "Curse of King Tut's Tomb!"

Archaeologists believe that the ancient Egyptians mummified more than 500 million bodies!

As only a few thousand mummies have been discovered, this means that hundreds of millions of mummies still lie beneath the Egyptian sands. If you're brave enough to face the curse of the mummies, maybe you can get a shovel and start digging!